CW00504511

About the Author

Ryleigh Lynch — Born in West Yorkshire in the 1960s; a 'milkman's daughter' who always had a passion for writing but spent most of her childhood years growing up in the 'naughty' corner. Ryleigh has spent most of her working life as an Operational Manager in the NHS. After a very turbulent marriage, she finally found the strength to leave and after decades once again turned to writing, which is how 'Dare to Dream' went from a dream to reality, and tells through verse that you can overcome adversity and find true happiness

RyleighLynch33@outlook.com

lots of love

Ryleigh Lynch x

xx

Dare to Dream

Ryleigh Lynch

Dare to Dream

Olympia Publishers
London

www.olympiapublishers.com
OLYMPIA PAPERBACK EDITION

A CIP catalogue record for this title is
available from the British Library.

ISBN: 978-1-78830-971-4

First Published in 2021

Olympia Publishers
Tallis House
2 Tallis Street
London
EC4Y 0AB

Printed in Great Britain

Dedication

This book of verses are written for and dedicated to the 'Specialness' in my life, my childhood friend whom I lost touch with for too many years and who then came back into my life; my Anam Cara. They are written about the gracious 'Specialness' of her which brought the 'possible' out of the 'impossible', how she gave me strength and courage, and whose faithfulness and loyalty together with her commitment, protection and dedication walked steadfastly with me on a journey to 'Dare to Dream'. 'Specialness' who gave me the greatest gift there is; she saved my life and after years of living a nightmare healed my despair, hurt, pain and loneliness and whose 'Specialness' gifted me my freedom, safety, peace, tranquillity, and happiness. Lynn ('Robyn') — without you there would be no me, and without me there would be no verses and no realisation of 'our' 'Dare to Dream' which is now 'our' message to others to never give up hope, to 'Dare to Dream' and that you can come out of the darkness into the light and find happiness and your own piece of 'Specialness'.

Thank you

I love you

Acknowledgements

In memory of my beautiful mum, whose love of life and beautiful smile I still miss each and every day; who was my mum, best friend and sister all rolled into one and whose love and devotion to me had no bounds. My beautiful mum who taught me many, valuable lessons in life, and to live and love life, and to show kindness and caring towards others. I miss you, Mum, I love you.

Dad, thank you for loving me as you do. I may not have been the dancer you were hoping for and I certainly didn't thank you for me having to get up at 4 a.m. to deliver the milk every morning before school, but you taught me hard work and ethical values that have got me through life and I know you are proud of me — I love you, thank you.

Ashley and Leah, my two gorgeous beautiful children. I am so proud of you both; two caring individuals, who are my life. Thank you for loving me as you do and for being the two brilliant bright shining stars in my life who I love unconditionally and make my life complete and worth living. I love you both.

My gorgeous daughter-in-law, Ady, who has brought so much happiness into my life and my beyond beautiful grandkids, Evie, Freya, and our new handsome addition, Noah. I love you all unconditionally, thank you.

My big brother, Antony, who has always looked after his 'little sis' and still does. We shared an incredible childhood filled with treasured times and memories which now as adults we still make and share. Mum's 'favourite' (well that's what I believed), but who is everyone's favourite, how can you not be? You are a kind hearted, generous, compassionate, gentle, caring, and loving individual who is my incredible brother. Always my protector and who has always been so caring supportive and loving but has gone above and beyond during these last hard and difficult couple of years, thank you, I love you so much.

Sue, my precious gorgeous sister-in-law, for loving and caring for me throughout the years — and who isn't a sister-in-law but in my eyes is my sister, whose generosity, love and guidance have been invaluable, keeping me strong and focused. I love you, Sue.

Hannah, Naomi, Paul and John, my gorgeous nieces and nephews who I love and adore with all my heart, and their insatiable zest for life, I am so proud of you all.

To my extended family; Janet, Pete, Mitch, Joelle and Brandon. What can I say; when I found Lynn again after so many years, I didn't just gain Anam Cara and her specialness, but I gained the special love of you all. You have accepted me with open arms and smothered me with so much love. Thank you for all the wonderful, brilliant and treasured times we have shared and the ones we will continue to share. Thank you for your love and acceptance of me through some difficult times and for your devotion to my happiness, I love you all.

Jean and Steve, treasured friends who have always 'had my back'. For your friendship, love and protection. For the years of treasured memories, the thousands of miles we have shared on runs through the streets and the hills of Yorkshire, and of course, the London Marathon. I love you both so much, thank you.

Gordon and Skye, thank you for coming into my life. For showing me so much kindness caring and love. For your love and support helping me through this last year. Thank you for loving me as you do. For your understanding, your patience, your generosity and for loving and accepting me for me. Thank you, I love you both, and of course not forgetting the recent new addition into the fold, Luna(tick).

Thank you to Collette, who was one hell of a boss — but who wasn't just a boss but became a valued friend who got me back on track; I love you.

Pauline, Steve and Andrea; thank you, my running pals, for being valued friends, I love you.

In memory of a special childhood friend who I lost last year and of our crazy childhood and the treasured times which we shared, Bozzie, I love and miss you my friend

To all my friends and colleagues in my life that have kept me focused and smiling, thank you I love you all.

Introduction

'Dare to Dream' is the telling of my life changing journey, a journey from darkness to light, a journey I thought to be impossible. Each verse has been written in dedication to a very special person, the person who shared this journey with me, the person who changed my 'impossible' to 'possible', my lifelong friend, my Anam Cara.

Our special friendship began fifty-two years ago in a school playground, Robyn simply walked up to me, 'shoved me', grinned and said 'Wanna be my friend? That was it; our friendship was sealed and we became inseparable from that moment on — well, apart from when we had to go home for tea and to bed of course. We were mischievous, very much so, but Robyn had the face of an angel so she always managed to get away with things, whereas I was a hot-headed ginger, who spent most of my junior school life stood in the corner with my hands on my head. We could run like the wind, had no fears, always up for a dare, were the only kids in our village who could leap frog standing up; from sun-up to sun-down we were on a constant 'go, go, go,' and no matter where we were or what we were doing our days were always filled to the brim with fun, laughter and happiness, we hadn't a care in the world.

Eventually though school life had to end, it was time for us to both get jobs. Sadly this was when we lost touch and went our separate ways; unbelievable I know, after so many years of being so close, but fate dictated we had to part, so part we did. I never forgot Robyn and spent years on social media searching different sites trying to find her, but with no luck. Then on 27th June 2016, a local link randomly popped up on my computer. I pressed the link, typed in her name and up popped a photo of Robyn at one of her birthday parties with me in it as well! I couldn't believe it, after so many years of searching I'd finally found her. I immediately sent her a message asking if she remembered me, she answered me back straight away. We began chatting and I found out Robyn had also been searching for me which is why she had put the photograph up on the site in the hope that I would see it. She'd also thought to add her maiden name, knowing that I wouldn't know her married name.

Our friendship kicked off again right where we'd left it, but little did we know that our friendship would soon evolve into Anam Cara, two souls as one. We had both led very different lives; I married someone who worked in the chemical industry, who was into soul music and a scooter boy. Robyn had taken herself off to California, where she married into a family from the movie and TV industry. How different our marriages were, Robyn's was filled with sunshine, beaches and laughter; mine was a dark secret that no-one knew about, a lie that I lived. To the outside world it looked perfect, two kids, a nice house, I had a good job, it couldn't be better than that, could it? But behind closed doors it was a whole different story. It was years of control, physical and mental abuse. Part of his control was making friends with my friends on Facebook, which he did with Robyn. He of course tried to break our friendship up, he even tried to scare her off a few times but it didn't work, she saw through him right from the 'get-go'. After a particular beating, Robyn somehow read between the lines of my message and picked up on something. She wouldn't outright ask me, but I knew she had an inkling — it was time for me not to live a lie anymore, I could finally tell the truth.

Robyn wasn't happy of course knowing that someone she cared so deeply about was being treated this way, and from that day forward, she made it her quest that I wouldn't live life like that anymore. She would open my eyes to the fact that it wasn't right, that I needed to understand and see there was a better life out there, so with her kid gloves she took me by the hand and with baby steps led me to where I am now; a new life, in a new home, surrounded by love, happiness and peace.

I always enjoyed writing and dreamed of one day writing a book. Robyn released the confidence in me to start writing again, so I started to write verses, which were to try and thank her for everything she had done for me and about the journey we both shared. Robyn thought my verses were also a form of 'self-therapy' and encouraged me to continue writing them. It's extraordinary, really, the journey we have shared, often thousands of miles apart; how she's taken me from someone who wanted to end their life because I felt my life had no meaning, to the complete opposite now. I'm back to being that kid again, happy, carefree and fun loving.

Robyn and I met after so many years on 29th September 2016, a truly magical time, and we have met many times since as she comes home to England every year. Finding Robyn also means I now have a beautiful extended family. I have always been terrified of flying but in March 2020 I put my fears aside to realise my dream of visiting Robyn in California. Sharing Robyn's journey through our lost years, a truly special and magical time. Welcome to our journey, a journey that taught me it is okay to… 'Dare to Dream'.

My Voice

Through my verses is the voice of the words I can't find or speak, that talk of the days gone by so dark oh so bleak

Of the feelings of loneliness being scared at times feeling a freak, and of course of the specialness in my life so beautiful so Angelique

As the words start to form and swiftly fall into verse, they release emotions that once were my curse

Of the times I lived to the wire two young kids hardly nothing in my purse, sinking, drowning under water totally submerged

When I write it releases all the tears that have formed around my broken heart, tears for my specialness who came back and gave me a brand new start

Tears that flow at the enormity she went through to save me how huge was her part, in piecing together all of me so shattered as my life had been blown apart

Yes at times I feel broken sad and bad, that I'd placed so much of my life on her but broad are her shoulder pads,

This verse is my acceptance I know she did that to get me away from all the bad I had, and who showed me to write in verse shows it wasn't me that was the one that was mad

Advice

Specialness that gave me advice and opinions that made me stop and think, I would often sit at the table take stock as I poured yet another drink

My mind began to start to question my life of routine tied to the kitchen sink, one which in all honesty had taken me to the brink

I didn't understand that so many things were wrong, I just thought I'd caused the beatings he was maybe a little headstrong

How stupid was I to think that was normality the control I lived with all day long, until my specialness came back and said that isn't normal it is not where you belong

My smile was false and had faded through the passing of time, my laughter too was false I hid it well in the right places I'd chime

Specialness that saw through that saw my soul had lost its rhyme, tenderly showed me I needed to go on a journey with many hills to climb

A journey we shared with her taking me away from my dark scary place, supporting my baby steps with her loving and her grace

Who brought me back into the light helped me unpack my case, specialness that brought the old me back and the biggest true smile on my face

Nothing for Free

They say nothing comes for free in life, well I can prove them wrong, the greatest gift this world has seen cost nothing and has been in my life all along

It is a specialness as beautiful as the morning bird song, a wonderful, courageous and magical force that is tall and oh so strong

How do I know this, come listen a while, I had a dark secret, no-one would I tell, caught in a nightmare of a violent lifestyle

And when I thought there's no point going on, this is no life, it's nothing worthwhile, crash bang wallop came a magnificent force all wrapped up in an incredible smile

Been a few years hasn't it my friend since we ran, laughed and walked as one, well, have no fear my soul heard your cry no way in this world are you done

So walk in my shoes follow my footsteps and at times we will have to run, but trust me through the battles ahead have faith we will not be outdone

And so I followed the beam of my specialness's light, we climbed mountains high as we knocked obstacles out of sight

Until the day everything black had turned pure white and the promise of peace, comfort and happiness was there I was transported into my specialness daylight

I Found

I found my childhood special friend, specialness that I thought I'd lost, searched high and low through the valleys and fields, the oceans I did cross

All was not in vain, I found her once more and with that came the demise of my holocaust, the life so controlled and rigid no longer surrounded by frost

I'm back to hold your hand she said, wipe away the tears you shed and I do that why, because I am your friend, I'm here to protect, keep you safe, I am your bookends

Gone now will be the life you've lived one I could never comprehend, I will reignite the spark in you have no fear I'm with you now until the bitter end

No longer will you feel sad and down for your smile will return, the twinkle that once lived in you will rise again and brightly burn

I will sit with you for how many hours it may take, share each and every one of your concerns, listen to all of your hopes and dreams all of which you yearn

And so the weeks, months and years went by with my specialness by my side, a long and arduous journey, a long and bumpy ride

Defeating each obstacle along the way, every minute I was with her just filled my heart with pride, so returned happiness and contentment that her magic gave to me a new and wonderful world she gave me with her arms so open wide

No End

When there seemed no end to the hurt that I felt, all the pain of the blows that left deep open welts

Like a robot getting on with life, after all these were the cards you were dealt, but as the years passed and I was sinking, overwhelmed and going into a total melt

No focus, no vision dark and dismal, no belief all washed out to sea, caught in the storm of the waves that gripped tight at me

Where am I going, the rain that is pouring is screaming for help it continued to be a silent plea, this is it no hope, forever as this though it shall be

Then a bright light appeared along the crest of the waves, beaming its light steering the way

It was my specialness back in my life, my strong tall lighthouse, no longer scared I was suddenly brave, ahead was her lifeboat she was back to protect me, my life she will save

And as she threw the lifebuoy my way, she smiled her beautiful smile saying I'm back no longer, are you washed out to sea lost in the fog

So my specialness rescued me, cleared and led the way out of my darkened smog and took me into a life of happiness both together with one hell of a giant leap frog

Together

So many memories together we do share, some the best times and some just total nightmares

There are things that only we both know, onto each other could we impart, an unbroken bond which means that for each other we are always there

But in a friendship so strong, happy, loving and versatile, you've always had that specialness that takes you that extra mile

Which is why you kept me focused and strong and on our journey kept me in file, until you opened the gate to happiness and gave me the gift to once again smile

Of Course

Of course I tried to understand how it had come to be, that the person I once had been was now no longer me

I searched high and low to find a cause but of course I was unable to see, that the one person I thought loved me in sickness and in health, had me locked in the control of his world and thrown away the key

We were the perfect couple, two kids and everything that the package did show, but behind the mask that I wore, little did anyone know

If I was an actress then I would win an Oscar, the world at my feet aglow, the reality of it all was the opposite with each and every blow

I was the greatest makeup artist you could ever meet, the most patient agony aunt for every time he did cheat

It was never going to happen again, things would change life would again be sweet, just to show me he meant every word of course I'd get a treat

But they too were not what you would wish to receive, the packages once opened of objects just made me want to heave

Screaming inside if you love me why do you so deceive, oh how I wish I could stop this life get up find the strength to leave

There was and should have been an ending but not a happy one, the mask and make up I wore were melting, there's no way out my time here is done

But that wasn't to be the ending because out there was an ear to listen, out there was someone, specialness that would save me who would and could not be outdone

No longer was I locked away in the darkness of my despair, for forth came a light with a force so bright and flames so fierce that tore through my snare

Specialness who stripped down each and every evil layer, until I found true happiness where I am now, yes at last I'm walking on air

Specialness That

Specialness that caught and took the rainbows to shine throughout my rain, colours so bright and vibrant that did erase my pain

Specialness that had the strength to stop me from falling, taking all the strain, gave me the vision and belief to believe I could start all over again

Specialness that climbed mountains to get me on the right track, relentless energy that kept me going she was such a power pack

Specialness that kept me focused told me follow your dreams never look back, a wonderful beautiful specialness who is the most precious beautiful gift there is, there is no doubt about that

For Years

For years I lived behind a painted smile just like a circus clown, that gave a performance to my audience wherever, in every city and town

The shoes I wore were far too big which is why I always fell down, the suit I wore was ragged and torn, like me a hand-me-down

I tried of course for the smile on my face to spread inside my heart, but the pain and destruction of the life that I had meant they were just spare parts

But the show must go on, I can't let my audience see me fall apart, that of course as always will wait until they have finally gone, they depart

The trombone I had was missing some notes a fine tune was what was needed, for years it had been playing the same song which became totally unheeded

The balloons I did carry had all shrivelled their sell by date well exceeded, too many obstacles in the way my act how it was impeded

Until a new act came to town, magical specialness crashing on her trapeze through the big top, who gathered me up to join in her act don't worry no longer will you fall I won't let you drop

The audience were now on their feet in awe 'woah' to the finale you could hear a pin drop, and high she threw me into the air of somersaults my smile and heart connecting together in happiness finally together, forever non-stop

Another Night

Another night is over and as the sun goes down, I think and look up to the stars wondering where my specialness is, is she still wearing her crown

The kids are all tucked up in bed safe in their dreams gone are the frowns, their mum is still with them, another day she didn't drown

Daybreak is upon us and so the sun does rise let's see what today will bring, kids dropped off to school racing in as the bell did ring

See you later my lovelies as I hug and kiss them goodbye so they do cling, have a wonderful day I say, I love you whatever the day may bring

And so the routine of the days and years did pass me by, living a façade of the smiles that hid inside of how I did cry

But I always looked up into the bright blue sky, made a wish that one day my specialness would be back once more, close, nearby

Little did I know that fate would play such a part in what would be a new incredible start

That one wish I had held for so long close to my heart, was back, specialness that saved my life and gave me the happiness that stopped me from falling apart

Finding

Finding the road to happiness was not an easy one, it's hard to contemplate what I went through with my specialness, a war that we both won

And as I sit in the garden of life so green and open wide under the warmth of the sun, my specialness smiles that beautiful smile and says come, let's reflect on what we have done

I want to paint you a picture she said, one that will open your heart, the colours I choose as I paint will create the steps we took from the very start

My brush will be the strokes that will cover the darkness of the canvas that played such a part, of filling your life for far too many years before you had the courage and strength to depart

The oils I choose will not run as the rivers of tears that you shed, the water I clean it with will wash away the infection of where you once bled

Each colour I use and evenly spread, will be vibrant like autumn, no longer dark and dismal like the turmoil that lived in your head

The oranges, reds, greens, purple and blues will replace the blacks and greys of the hatred that was the cause, and as I looked at my specialness in awe did I pause

At the beauty of the masterpiece in front of me her brushes tidied back into her vase, and the wonderment of what she had given me for which there can never be enough applause

Looking Back

When I look back how strange it is to see who I am now to what I used to be, they say time is a great healer or so is the decree

But the reason I am where I am now is not the passing of years that's so clear to see, but because of my specialness and what she did and gave to me

Oh yes I would burst into laughter but no one could see the pain, or know of the abuse that upon me did rain

At times there'd be tears and such torture inside my brain, all telling the tale of how my life was in vain

I showed a side of me people wanted to see, living a lie for far too long, headlights of the car crash of my life hitting me full on

Hopes and dreams still remained deep within but they seemed a fantasy all just so wrong, how my heart and soul wanted not to weep but instead burst into song

And just like the fairy-tale I always held close to my heart, so that materialised into reality when my specialness came back, so radiant and bright my world no longer black

With an energy and determination so strong she lifted me up into her special backpack, to a journey of adventure that had its ups and downs, until we reached the end that my specialness got me to who I am now to bring my life back on track.

Wish Upon a Star

When you wish upon a star your dreams come true, and all mine came true thanks to the specialness of you

Living life so alone, so desolate, so blue, trapped in a life I thought was the norm as the years passed by and flew

I thought of my specialness many times and wished I could have her there through the sad lonely nights, to talk to and listen to, turn the wrongs into rights

I needed my specialness but I'd lost her, or so I thought was my plight, until that wonderful day she came back into my life and gave me the strength to fight

She told me I know you've had to survive and cope all on your own, but I'm back now my friend no longer are you alone

So then began a journey each hour of each day and the seeds of freedom were sown, every web of darkness around me bit by bit the cobwebs were broken and blown

Lessons

Since my specialness has returned I've learned so many lessons she is the greatest teacher by far, without which I would still be living and stuck inside of that dreadful tar

She taught me to be true to myself and not stay trapped in that ugly jar, of the life I had been subjected to that had inflicted each one of my scars

I learned there was a life in me that didn't have to bear all the pain and destruction that had become my daily snare, I could leave the life I had that was my daily nightmare

The strength is there inside you she told me and I'm here for you to share, all that has happened to you none of which is fair

So as I sat and listened and learned a thing or two, so the confidence that was inside me suddenly it grew

With each bell that called the end of my lesson my homework I would do, and return for the next one soaking in everything I was learning about myself and life through and through

And as exam time approached so the nerves kicked in, don't be scared my friend it's inside you now don't get yourself in a spin

As the clock of time passed of our journey the lessons were truly built in, and I passed with flying colours thanks to my specialness and the lessons she had taught which found me the freedom of my happiness now deep within

Birds of a Feather

The meaning of true friendship is what we have together, two souls as one, yes two birds of a feather

Specialness that is our Anam Cara enjoying life as it should be whatever the weather, never again will we be apart we will always be together

Only we both know the true meaning of our friendship, the highs and the lows, the journey we've shared together only both of us will ever know

But throughout all the laughter and tears, you were there constantly to hold my hand as we conquered my fears

There's still a journey ahead as we both know but gone are the darkest years, my specialness pulled me through, I salute you my precious friend, thank you, cheers

Now

Now that I have the vision and eyes that do see, just makes me realise the magnitude of what you've done and given to me

I may have worn a smile on the outside but in my heart there lived no glee, a life that was like branches broken from a beautiful oak tree

Living day by day with words thrown at me with hatred that was so raw, am I that bad an individual will the ice of the expletives ever thaw

Is this for real so said my mixed-up head, one minute it's love the next my upper jaw, so many emotions it's crazy this life jigsaw

Then one day came a brightness just like diamonds in the sky, my specialness has returned I gave one almighty sigh

Through my silence she knew and read there were many tears to dry, that she had to take me on a journey that would kiss my darkness goodbye

Integrity is her middle name that restored my faith, gave me back my dignity, this is not who you should be my friend you deserve a better life one that isn't so uncomplimentary

Follow me I'll lead the way and gone will be the life that has been your debility, so with my specialness hand in hand she led me through the doors of happiness oh how life is lived now so very differently

Count on

Specialness I can count on and specialness I can trust, that came to me when I had fallen, picked me up wiped away all the darkened dust

A brilliance of light that came back into my life with an almighty gust, leading the way to my freedom with her magical stardust

Trust and security which gave me a sense of peace, and with each step I took held my hand and so the fear began to cease

As hard and stressful it seemed at times so did come my release, to a new world of happiness created by my specialness, her wonderful masterpiece

Deep

Specialness that came back to me and helped me put my past to rest, a broken individual that had been reduced to a mess

Specialness that heard my soul calling took me in flight to her nest, and from that moment on I knew I'd be safe oh how I was blessed

Like a fallen tree, branches dead and broken, through them I heard you whisper to me she said, is this the tree that I once knew whose tears like sap she does shed

The tree that blossomed and flowered that was never dead, side by side as children, free to grow only happiness was inside your head

Ashamed of what my life had become I hung my head in shame, don't you dare do that my friend for you are not to blame

I will heal all your scars bring your darkness to light no longer will your walk be lame, then on a journey we shall go an adventure that will reignite your flame

True to her word she stayed by my side no longer did I weep, each day brought a bit more strength no longer did I feel left on the heap

Until the day the door opened up to happiness that was complete, the roots of our past and the friendship we shared had never gone it couldn't be broken it runs too deep

Comrade

Specialness that has been there helped me through the bitterness of my life so bad, my precious friend that has been loyal and true, the perfect comrade

No longer alone no one to share my hopes and dreams with no longer a nomad, my specialness was back in my life now back to mend the broken scars and all that was sad

Specialness that helped me find that lost kid from many years ago, who listened to my heartache all the despair that did outflow

We are now Anam Cara with a bond that can't be broken so much gusto, true friends forever, wherever together as one we go

Wondered

I have often sat and wondered had questions in my head, the whys and wherefores from morning until I took myself to bed

Many years I searched all over so many books I sat and read, but I couldn't find the answers was it me, maybe I didn't understand had probably misread

As the days of the years continued to roll on by, his anger became a harsh daily persistence as did the intensity of the evil in his eye

I wore a mask, one that shielded the reality of my life, which each day I would apply, and it seemed that the only escape was for me to say to life farewell and goodbye

And when the darkness was coming to a close a presence I thought I'd lost came back as bright as could be, specialness that wore such a beautiful smile shouted out yes my friend guess what it's me

Craziness that took my hand said just look ahead and see, out there is a wonderful world and guess what it's our own personal shopping spree

Since then my specialness has brought me so many wonderful gifts, showered me with precious things she is a spendthrift

All what she gives me is priceless as she goes on her way wherever she drifts, but the most priceless of all is the specialness of her presence and love that is my lifeline which is one hell of a happiness lift

There Is

There is a certain specialness that turned my world around, specialness that can't be bought or sold it's so rare but luckily I found

Who picked me up from the years that I had been knocked deep into the ground, cleared the dirt thrown onto me that had become my compound

Who untied the knots that were the grounding of the thoughts inside my mind, opened my eyes to the things that were wrong to which I was so blind

Specialness who opened my soul to hers so we'd become one become combined, restarted the handles on the clock of opportunity so once again they did wind

Tenderness that brought me into the light from my shadow, who eradicated every scar each and every woe

Courage and strength that was my shield so I could leave get up and go, and on the journey we shared, like a river her specialness did flow

Who crushed all my fears so deeply hidden that I didn't understand had misunderstood, turned the negativity of my life showed me not no I can't but that yes I could

Specialness that I'd shared years of carefree happiness with throughout our childhood, specialness that came back brought me back happiness she is the greater the good

Vibrant

Specialness that came back to me as she landed vibrant colours, they did flash, strong courageous and mighty who put out my flames the remains just ash

No longer did I have to live life have to suffer the backlash, or the daily allergy of despair that was in me like a constant rash

Brightly sparkling such a beautiful shining star, inviting me into her galaxy her aide memoir

A journey, one that would take a while as it would be long and go on so far, one on which she would fiercely protect and look out for me like a steely jaguar

Nothing could match her power on that journey we would share, whenever we turned a corner hit an obstacle, she was always there

The times she had to open me up to the truth of the whys to my despair, how it hurt her to have to do that but she did with tenderness and care

Specialness whose determination waved her magic wand, took me to a happier place yes that and more totally beyond

To realise her dream for my safety security and happiness she's certainly not dim but yet blonde, specialness that now builds and fills my life with treasured memories together forever Anam Cara is our special bond

No Need

No need for any more questions my specialness said to me, for your memories are now your pictures for today, the bits of you that were broken and damaged are healed so you can enjoy each and every day

Yes those broken pieces were experiences of the truth that life shouldn't be that way, but that's behind you now you aren't going back to that darkness believe me no way

There will still be some sadness but that will be for family or friends close to you who were everything, but latch onto the wonderful times you shared the memories they did bring

Close your eyes think of them and you find they are not far away you'll hear them sing, you'll see their smile such cherished memories that will become a beautiful thing

Shadow

I had a shadow watching over me one that took complete control, that carefree happy person I was, was taken away, I was no longer whole

A shadow who from the front such a gentleman a rose stuck in his buttonhole, but from the back a monster emerged kept me caged and was on constant patrol

Darkness of the shadow that got into the corners of my mind, moulded me by fear in what he had planned had designed

Over the days, months and years my vision slowly dwindling to become totally blind, goodbye to the wishes I prayed for that things would change that I would wake up and he'd be kind

But then one day the shading of the shadow changed, where had all the darkness gone this is weird it's really strange

As I continued to look a beautiful vision came into range, it was the shadow of my specialness I thought I had lost but she was back the evidence was there as hellos were exchanged

With gentle eyes that shone so bright and her gorgeous beautiful smile, many years have passed she said but I heard your soul travelled from across the isle

You've had a very dark shadow that has given you a life on trial, but it's time to end all of that for you to see that life is worthwhile

Step into my shadow now my friend and you will see not all are dark with no air, put your trust in me no need to be afraid or beware

I have some gifts to give you long overdue I know but to you

I can now share, they are the vision and belief you can have happiness that people love you, yes they care

My specialness gathered me up took me on a journey only both of us will know, defeated the shadow as he tried to stop us in our tracks but her light was too strong and too bright was her glow

And with each step my vision and belief became clearer and my strength and courage did grow, as the shadow now watching over me brought me back the happiness that we both shared together all those years ago

Just Can't See

Specialness that can't see just how special she is at all, specialness who is that graceful dancer that lights up all the dance halls

Such specialness that comforts you with her beautiful loving shawl, who knows when you need her always hears your call

Thoughtful kind and giving never wanting anything in return, the extinguisher that puts out the flames that surround you that burn

Who only wants your safety and happiness that is her primary concern, specialness with her beautiful smile who gave me a purpose a life and somewhere to turn

Do You Know

Do you know how tall I stand, as high as the trees all thanks to the specialness of you, and now my branches are filled with blossoms with the sweetest smell it's true

Now stood in a beautiful garden not the cemetery of the life I once knew, out with nature and the fields of opportunity which are now my landscape my view

How your specialness has changed the persona the DNA in me, taught me to be my true self gave me the strength that set me free

Who showed me how to laugh again be reckless, mischievous happy and carefree, specialness whose kindness and caring unlocked and opened up a whole new world with her special magical key

Every Night

Every night I would go to my bed switch off all the lights, hoping that when I switch them back on like their images my life would be bright

But that never happened because nothing was lily white, the only certainty I had was the hurt the pain and fright

A lifetime alone tossing to and fro no one to trust, my resilience fading as I got older it was now beginning to rust

Those eyes would look once more at me filled with hatred and disgust, time to take another beating but I've learnt to take it, adjust

Then all of a sudden there came a power surge, just when I was about to give up teetered on the verge

A force so powerful a vibrant blinding light was its energetic upsurge, and with it a spark was ignited and then two souls did merge

My specialness was back and gave me her oath that my life would change in every way, no more darkness or sorrow would fill each and every one of my days

A chariot of specialness that took me on a journey defeated my prey, brought me untold happiness specialness that is such a beautiful glorious ray

Puppet

So long I was a puppet but I didn't dance or sing, I had no control to how my moves would be because I was pulled by his strings

My parts were all broken worn out not worth anything, my show never had a happy ending only sadness that my puppeteer did bring

There never was a hop, skip or tap in my feet, because the music that played was to a rhythmless beat

The audience would look in wonder no claps would come from their seats, there would be no encore or a cry for a repeat

I tried to change the story I did with all my might, but the strings that held me were too rigid too tight

The show would be over I folded back into my box for the night, darkness as always would descend on me and so would my fright

But then one day I was unfolded and taken out of my box, the lightness appeared complete with a new outfit head to toe to my socks

I had a new puppeteer a specialness who was wearing her magical docs, and happy music blasted out from a big bright noisy jukebox

Dance my little puppet no longer do you have to hide, for now you are no longer alone I am here forever by your side

I've given you new strings, and with a hop, skip and jump you will now glide, no more control with me for you there will only be happiness and pride

And I have something more special because I have given you

a heart, no longer a puppet those years have gone they can now depart

You now have the vision and belief that the life as it was you no longer are a part, and so the love of my specialness cut my puppet strings that brought me a whole new wonderful start

So Far Away

Specialness that lives so far away, but that doesn't stop her specialness not one bit not in any way

The brightness of her smile crosses the thousands of miles meaning my days are never dull or grey, her presence all around so happiness prevails each and every day

Specialness that surrounded me through my troubles, anxiety and woe, the blanket of her specialness steadfast wherever I was did go

Darkness has no place so strong is the essence of her glow, that nurtured my scattered seeds so they could blossom and grow

Special lessons she taught me to never give in, no longer had I to accept my life keep taking it on the chin

That showed me the way and the strength a journey to begin, a battle ahead but one together we would conquer and would win

Specialness with tender loving hands who was there for her friend in need, whose protection and determination unshackled my chains so that I was finally freed

And as she promised me that was her wish was her creed, to bring me safety security and happiness and boy did she succeed

Gave Me

Specialness that gave me a voice to ask the questions, times before I couldn't I just wouldn't dare, who took my hand sat down with me as I relived the years of my living nightmare

Specialness that looked at me with such tenderness and care, and said I know at times you've asked yourself the whys and said that it's not fair

I will mend your broken pieces and the negativity will fade will go, your vision and belief will reappear and the positivity will open and will flow

The path I pave for you will lead to your happiness chateaux, which will be surrounded by fields of vibrant flowers that will blossom as they grow

Now it's time for our journey to take you where you should be and belong, I will protect you give you the courage and I will keep you strong

Stay by my side keep focused and positive and we won't go wrong, and I promise you the day will come when you will hear the birds singing their beautiful song

Specialness that kept her promise to me kept me on the right track, erased all my demons wiped out the negativity so I looked forward never back

Who tended and cleansed all my wounds, closed up each and every crack, a gift of specialness that I have in my life wrapped up in a wonderful beautiful specialness pack

Darkest Hours

Through my darkest hours I would sit alone with my tears and wonder why, how come I didn't have the strength to stop living such a wasteful lie

But I didn't have the knowledge or have the answers as a new day would dawn, so again a false smile I would apply, and resign myself to the torture living with that nightmare of a terrible guy

I'd search for the magic that would realise my prayers, but they never came each day would end with anger and hatred as he'd blow he'd flare

Of course no one would listen or believe me, he told me so you had better beware, if you try and break the chain on your own head be it I swear

I was like an animal caught in a trap, the fortress that was home too thick had no opening no gap

Everyone else thought he was a lovely caring reliable chap, little did they know his favourite pastime was giving me a slap

But one day the walls to the fortress came crashing down, an army of specialness that was to be his downfall, his knockdown

Specialness who had the know-how, courage and strength so his reign she did drown, specialness that saved me and turned my life around

Once Again

You are so very special to me and I'm struggling to find the words to say, everything in my head is all muddled up and I can't get my verse out as hard as I try come what may

I know you will understand and forgive me although I feel your specialness I have betrayed, but well I guess it's because I'm just having one of those full on crappy days

And I know you can see through me, know my hurt and pain, know all of my mixed up feelings that are going around inside my brain

I love you my Anam Cara, your specialness and it's magic lives in my being every one of my veins, which means I'll be back later on with my verses back on track and with the specialness of you once again

Looked

Specialness that looked through me saw that I was not okay, that knew the clouds had come into my blue sky so now they were becoming grey

Who saw in my eyes the struggles that had developed and misted my ray, who knew the light was starting to fade on the brightness of my days

Specialness whose smile took hold and told me keep strong, that I would make it through, whose hand would be there for me holding the bucket to catch the tears I would spew

Specialness that reached out when I struggled once more to the questions I asked to which I had no clue, but I didn't need to go far to find the answers because my specialness gave them to me because she is special through and through

Not Knowing

Specialness that saw me faltering not knowing where to go, saw my struggles of the days gone by and knew I was down at an all-time low

Who could see into my mind that my thoughts were muddled they just couldn't flow, whose specialness swept into action to get this show back on the road reignited by her glow

Time for my winds of change to work its magic she said, as they took me like a feather floating on the breeze as her calmness did spread

Stopping me from falling back down into that dark hole of dread, making sure I didn't fall backwards only steps forward would be the ones I would tread

Specialness whose tenderness reached out and brought me right back on track, not with any fancy tricks like pulling a rabbit out of a hat

Hearing the words of my silence my tone that had gone completely flat, said come let's set the table same as always nothing has changed same number of chairs and placemats

But words are not important, it's what's in your heart and soul who and what you always had beside you, specialness steadfast in her promise who is always there with her specialness and love to pull me through

Nightfall

Nightfall is approaching and we are still sat on her magical swing, the day has been filled with laughter and tears but untold happiness above everything

The road is different now not insurmountable, just now and then the bumps that life does bring, I've been so lucky that my specialness came back brought me to the joy of what my heart now does sing

And as she's just reminded me the dreams you wish for you can achieve, always look forward not back to your life where only nothing you did receive

Specialness who gave me a new life one for years she carefully did plan and weave, which I now share with her and as we both continue to swing I know no way now can I not believe

Swing

Specialness that sat me down on her swing took my hand gently catching the tears that did fall, who looked at me with her beautiful smile said you are not alone no not at all

I know you are cold inside there's a chill here let me wrap you in the warmth of my shawl, time for us to take some more baby steps to replace your sadness your bounce we need to reinstall

With the sways of her swing quietness and calmness began to descend, the hurt and pain I felt her specialness working it's magic I was starting to mend

That dark place you lived in is gone it's your past that has come to a finish an end, but there will still be natural sadness that's how it is the reality of life my dear friend

With a gentle breeze as we continued to swing my tears still flowed my face wearing a frown, warmth and comfort surrounded me as the rays of the sun did beat down

You've completed a tough and hard journey where you lived is now a deserted town, you now have peace and happiness can be proud as you've turned your life totally around

The baby steps you now take are the ones to teach you the difference between natural sadness and what was your living nightmare, the tears from the sadness that fall from you now are for those for who you love and who care

Each baby step we now take are ones where we are completely and totally free no longer do we have to beware, specialness whose swing of life I sit on with my specialness and forever which I will share

Picture

We are going to draw a picture my specialness said, one like your life a dot to dot, the first lines we draw are the twists and turns of how it was yes each and every knot

The next lines we draw are the darkness all the despair and rot, a picture emerging don't worry still a long way to go much more for us to jot

These next dots of which there are many are the lines of the journey we shared, of the roads and paths we took when you were frightened and scared

Lines that depict your heartache of the nightmare you impaired, one we walked together on for miles and miles to get your broken pieces repaired

But these next dots are the curves of the corners that both of us turned, the flames there shown that destroyed your past which they burned

Each corner a sign showing the vision and belief in you that was making a return, of times we sat together and all of the lessons you learned

Not many dots left until the end now my lovely, only a few more to go, look how different these lines are because only happiness these do show

You are now in a valley of sunshine only brightness all around aglow, look the lines and dot to dots are complete showing the picture of how happy life does now flow

Difficult

Specialness who throughout our journey had to deal with times that were difficult and hard, watching over me day after day she was my own special bodyguard

Knowing about all of my nightmares how I was damaged and scarred, yet so far away from her friend who was so delicate brittle and charred

Specialness whose priority was my safety stop me falling through the net, making sure no matter what hour I was alright the okay being the green dot was set

Specialness whose giving knows no bounds that gave happiness and freedom to this brunette, specialness that has a heart of gold and a beautiful soul, the most special friend there is on this earth you could get

How Can I

How can I capture the traits of such specialness where do I begin, all her wonderful characteristics who she is on the outside through to within

The shield that surrounds her that deflects negativity no way will it ever break in, her personality larger than life so loud it deafens you with its din

Her beautiful smile like a lighthouse gives off light and shows you the right way to go, a smile that speaks a thousand words with its warmth and its glow

The spring in her step as she glides through life gracious as she flows, that has her audience mesmerised because she is life's greatest show

Her heart and soul know no bounds which she gives to those who she loves and cares, specialness who will fight with all of her might to end any living nightmares

Has a twinkle in her eyes mischievous at times when she is doing some 'watch me I dares', uniquely individual only one of her kind in her persona and what she does wear

Specialness whose tenderness is the only medicine you will ever need, that soothes all the hurt and pain of the open wounds that bleed

Who is the map of life when you're lost guides you onto the right path completely takes the lead, specialness that is so much more but one thing for sure yes she is beautiful specialness indeed

Inspiration

Specialness that is a wonderful inspiration who shares her gifts with me, has grown the blossom that now grows from the roots of my living tree

Gifts she shared to rebuild my soul to bring me happiness that was her guarantee, specialness who moved mountains so was her love and loyalty

The times she had to take my hand tell me things I didn't understand or know, how hard it hurt when she knew the truth for me would come as a shock a blow

Months and days of searching to find me the belief and vision the strength to pick me up from my low, hold me steadfast so I didn't fall when came the time to get up leave and go

Specialness who showed me I wasn't a statue or object, who was more than aware many times her honesty would take hold have an effect

Patiently through the months she knew I'd listen in my own time be able to see reflect, silently lovingly waiting for the right time to come and take me for my freedom to collect

Picking up my roots to my new world we both would explore, filled with fun and laughter no more darkness no not anymore

Her magical key that opened up nothing but vibrant colours through each and every door, special gifts she bestowed on me specialness who is special to the core

Dedication

Specialness whose dedication was given to me as a friend so true, a friendship that grew stronger with each day of the years that did accrue

A friend whose fun and laughter is infectious which ensures I'm never blue, she's one bat shit crazy individual with a heart of gold through and through

Her spirit that surrounds me as it has since we were kids, picking bluebells in the woods and as through the mud we slid

Who would stand up for me as the teachers would send me to the naughty corner sighing as they rolled their eyelids, who would let me copy her when I struggled with maths and fancy grids

Dedication that came back after losing too many years, I had lost the fun in life it had been replaced by too many tears

Her specialness that bounded back into my life filling it up again with cheer, who lifted me up fixed my pieces banished all of my fear

Precious love back to show me no more was I going to be alone, enveloping me once again like a tidal wave, a cyclone

Specialness that gave me strength courage vision and belief once more she was my backbone, and why I now have true happiness thanks to the biggest brightest specialness this world has ever known

Each Day

Specialness who each day puts a spring in my step and the biggest smile on my face, such a different story to the darkness that once invaded my every space

Gone are the days when I wouldn't know what was waiting for me how he'd be on my case, a force that controlled me and nearly destroyed me when I was in that awful place

But there came my specialness's beckoning that said follow me and I promise your freedom awaits, some things you won't know the meaning to but don't worry I'll explain and translate

So I took a deep breath as I went through that old and rusty gate, never to look back always forward she told me specialness that brought me my happiness thank you my soul mate

Stop

Specialness that took hold of me and said stop beating yourself up now you are coming out from your past, we are Anam Cara a friendship that is strong can't be broke made of steel to last

I know you are sorry about my love for you that you couldn't see and that your guilt is vast, but that doesn't matter to me as my love for you rose above that yes completely beyond it, it surpassed

As she tenderly looked at me with her beautiful smile erasing and clearing my frown, her love pierced my heart and told me I hadn't failed or let her down

Her specialness loud and clear the positivity striking my conscience stopping the drown, but that's my incredibly specialness my brilliant one in a million beautiful crazy special clown

Adventure

We are going on an adventure one day my specialness said, in search of all those hopes and dreams that are locked inside your head

It might take a while so you get packing and I'll make us some sarnies with the yummy crusty bread, then it's time to get outta here there are a few miles we have to tread

A wealth of knowledge and stories along the way she shared with me which became embedded within, the words from her book of wisdom was written with the ink beneath her skin

No longer would I live as I had the blows every day hit my chin, life was going to get better a battle ahead but one she said we would most definitely win

Along the way there will be a treasure hunt some prizes for you to collect, but what you'll find will not be gold in a form or be an object

Your prizes that you'll find will be vision and belief to which your heart and soul will connect, and the pieces of your past will become discarded be thrown away each one you will eject

At the end there will be a secret passage that will lead to a door to open that will need a magical key, behind that door will be the fields of life where you can run skip and jump be yourself be free

And my specialness she did lead me to that door which was the number thirty-three, which opened onto my happiness that my trust and belief in her and her specialness gave to me

How Often

How often I would sit alone and wish for another chance, to have that zest again inside me and for my heart to dance

Then I'd see something out of the corner of my eye that stare of his evil glance, then the room would fill of his mist and the darkness would descend as he'd advance

So many mistakes and failures selfishly I didn't want to be a constant loser but for once win, throw all the worn out objects of my life away open the lid cast them into the bin

My resilience was getting weaker it was time to give in, not a chance in hell mate not now I'm here came the words from my specialness's beautiful grin

Took my time coming back didn't I but better late than never, gone is the thunder and lightning from now on only sunshine will be the weather

My soul heard your calling, heard your pain seen the years of your endeavour, time to get moving my friend banish the sadness from your life for once, forever

Come it's time for a new beginning a new opening I have found, let's see who can run the fastest as she set off on a pace as she bound

The race went on for miles and miles at times my heart would pound, but there were no winners between us as we reach the end Anam Cara we were crowned

In the Dead of the Night

In the dead of night I heard a whisper it was my specialness telling me, that the time had come to make our move to our freedom for us to flee

Through the night we travelled many miles to reach the end no going backwards only forwards was the decree, and then my specialness said look here we are look there is our magical tree

I looked at this enormous tree so many branches all reaching into the clouds, come hurry up my specialness said it's there for us to climb as only we can because only we are allowed

I looked at the branches there were no buds but fruits some growing magical creatures whose chatter was persistent and loud, come quickly she said it's ours to explore that's good isn't it doesn't that make you feel proud

Together we began climbing the magical tree scaling up onto our first branch, it seemed so high up hell if we fall it will be just like an avalanche

Quickly she cried some of those creatures aren't nice as she squared up to them made a stance, they looked then scarpered they couldn't match her no way no they didn't stand a chance

We continued our climb up into the clouds nearly reaching the top then my specialness turned round looked at me and told me to halt to stop

Our climb has been long but this next bit is tough but hold onto me I promise I won't let you drop, and your reward will be sweet as through those clouds is the biggest there is in the whole wide world candy shop

We are reaching the land of birthdays come let's see what gifts await you, look there's three hurry open up let me see get the paper off without further ado

Out came three little gremlins each one pushing their way through, I'm conscience, I'm belief, I'm vision they shouted together in-situ

We are your gifts for the rest of your journey special gifts that your specialness has planned, and then we all set off walked through the clouds to Roundabout Land

A land like my past that had my head spinning where I had to live by his command, the same old song would play repeatedly with words that I couldn't stand

The lands we passed were plenty some scary and cold like ice and snow, the Rockling Land where you could only take one step forward without ten backwards so weary but my specialness kept me in tow

My belief telling me I could reach the end my vision helping me to see where to go, look we are just about there said my specialness it's the land of Take What You Want where everything is free her face lit up all aglow

Looking at me my specialness said what is it that has lived strong in all of your dreams, ask and it can now all be yours as her beautiful smile at me beamed

Happiness said my conscience with your special friend together by your side her light being your sunbeam, well your conscience can rest now your happiness enchanting wood awaits for you and your specialness now and forever in reams

Helped

Specialness that helped and saved me from years of feeling bad, calmed down the manic in me convinced me that I wasn't mad

Put the bounce into my step and the genuine smile back on my face no longer being sad, realised all my dreams I thought were impossible to reach, were just a fad

Who showed me not to be ashamed that she was with me so I was no longer alone, that I had been stunted with all I'd endured all at me that had been thrown

Beautiful specialness who was my priceless gemstone, who held my hand to take me on a journey which finally brought me back home

Turned To

Specialness that I turned to when my life was in a mess, not knowing which move to make each one a checkmate in a game of chess

I didn't have the answers of the whys and why nots the knowledge to address, the poison inside of me waiting to burst just like a gangrenous inflamed abscess

Specialness that came back to give my soul and spirit a lift, saw I no longer was carefree no zest it had gone out to drift

Who knew the time had come to change that, that she had to act swift, gather the tools and senses needed to save me which would become such a precious gift

So began the transition from the desolate soul I'd become, a whole new world began emerging one where I wasn't just existing feeling numb

Specialness that brought back laughter releasing me from the scrum, opened me up to the truth gave me the answers to what I had succumb

The countless times she held my hand caught my tears as she helped me face the seriousness of some things that had been, why there was so much darkness in my life and nothing was clean

Beautiful specialness that gave me a new life and happiness which for too many years it hadn't been, gave me the vision to see she would remain besides me to share this new world of our special evergreen

Now

Now I have a wealth of knowledge and there's been a change to my view, and there is only one reason for all of that which is of course the specialness that is you

Who bounded and bounced back into my life just like a manic kangaroo, who came to take me away from my darkness and pain be by my side as I made that first breakthrough

All the colours around me that were faded you brought back to life, severed the knots that kept me tied with the sharpness of your knife

Put me back together so that I could genuinely smile again got rid of all of my strife, your specialness who brought me happiness so that no longer will I live as that troubled beaten up wife

Streets Alone

The night was cold and dark as I wandered through the streets alone, the wind growing stronger the rain soaking me to the bone

Not sure where I was going startled by the ringing of my phone, it was him again no doubt checking where I was and why I wasn't home

I carried on walking until I reached a bridge beyond it was the glimmer of a light, intrigued I wandered closer until it was directly in my sight

It was coming from a house and when I looked through the window two kids were playing, laughing with all their might, carefree and happy the love so clear as they hugged each other tight

As I looked closer I took a sharp breath as it was my best friend and me, together when we were kids where life was filled with nothing other than happiness and glee

I heard her saying you and me are besties and forever that will be, nothing will ever come between us I'll always be there for you even when we are old and grey and have wobbly knees

The tears ran down my face those were such happy times and as I started to turn around, there she was stood saying I'm back to keep my promise my lovely how my heart beat so positively it did pound

Come she said it's time for us to go leave all your hurt and pain forever now in the background, because over that bridge is our journey to a much happier and safer ground

Rollercoaster

Life's a rollercoaster but not for the thrill of the ride, years spent living under the control of Mr Jekyll and Mr Hyde

A dark crazy world that I wished I could leave behind step outside, no end in sight to the violence and fear for it all to subside

Life has its ups and downs but the downs were constantly, until my specialness opened my eyes to everything that was done was wrongfully

Who gave me the strength to leave behind my life that was a catastrophe, specialness in all her glory who brought me happiness more than I dreamt could possibly be

Humpty Dumpty

Just like Humpty Dumpty that sat upon a wall, the ground was full of pieces from my one giant almighty fall

So many knocks I'd taken just like at the fairground in the coconut stall, no one could hear my cries for help because silent were my calls

A scattered giant puzzle now laid upon the floor, too hard to put back together looks like that's it I'm truly done for

Some swept under the carpet and some shoved to the back of the drawer, no more light only darkness no happiness nope no more

For years the drawer was locked tight and lost was the key, that crooked sinister smile said there's no escape that's a guarantee

But that smile started to fade when my specialness came back bigger and greater than Houdini, who planned my escape to perfection unlocked my chains to set me free

Magical specialness that found my missing pieces put them all back together again, brought back the ray of sunshine replacing my rain

Stopped the rot of the madness from making me insane, beautiful specialness that pumped the blood of happiness that now runs through my veins

Blessed

You know you are truly blessed when you find that special friend who knows everything you feel, why you are quiet as your tears fall the reason why knows what is real

Who understands reasons for your weaknesses because of the life you've had that to all others you did conceal, specialness who has the answers knows the way out which cards to give to deal

Yes I am truly blessed as I have a specialness so beautiful so rare, one I could turn to put my trust in with whom my troubles I could share

Specialness that conquered the control and evil that was steered by that ugly sinister stare, who like a Phoenix rose above to defeat the years of abuse that were my living nightmare

Then and Now

Specialness that is with me through the here and now and who was with me through the then, the then started as snotty nosed kids mischievously we'd hide in your den

Into our teens through the fields we would race and into the farm full of pigs and some hens, me asking to copy her as I struggled to write the answers to the exams with my pen

The then of happiness would come to a pause as the years rolled by sadly those days had come to an end, going into adulthood each our separate ways that would be the intend

The happiness I shared would dwindle be replaced by darkness that would so condescend, many nights I would fight to survive my being I would try to defend

Then the life was draining out of me but there remained one last drop, a force that would come back to me that would bring the rot to a stop

Specialness I had back then came back saying right it's time to make a change the 'then' I am here to swap, time to rid you of such evil for my forces will give them the chop

My then was taken on a journey a long one so it would be, and the then started to disappear replaced by the now which is happy and free

A now where I live my life realising my dreams with my specialness once again together carefree, a now with my beautiful specialness a wonderful now of that we both agree

Very Lucky

I am so very lucky I have a special presence that is with me every day, specialness that has given me so much in each and every way

Specialness that brought back the brightness into my life with her glorious beautiful ray, sunshine and laughter in abundance is now the life each and every day

Surrounded by a blanket that smothers me with love, a special friendship that was formed by that very first almighty shove

Nothing too much trouble every negativity and obstacle her specialness rises above, specialness so rare, precious and priceless she's unique only her there is one of

That special presence who every day puts a smile on my face, as her craziness and energy invades my every space

Her loving and giving which are this world's greatest showcase, her understanding, caring and tenderness which is her loving embrace

Specialness so mighty and strong means there's never can't but yes we will, where her psychic creativity is a god given talent and beautiful skill

I'm so lucky that I get to share all of that all of the specialness that over me she does spill, yes isn't life wonderful to have such specialness yes it's special and beyond brill

Replaced

Specialness that replaced my weakness with strength, said you can rise above this yes you can, hatred and control is not a life not for you and definitely not given to you by that man

I have been giving you the belief and vision which is there so you can live out that plan, comfort peace and happiness is what should be yours should be your lifespan

I've been repairing your broken pieces and these wings I have made for you, that will help you reach the sky through the clouds to the tranquillity so blue

You are not alone my presence will guide and help you through, and she wasn't wrong because I reached my paradise and dreams with my specialness so beautiful so true

Determination

Specialness whose steely determination showed me what life is all about, that quenched the thirst that lived in me for years that had been my drought

Such specialness whose love and presence wrapped around me became my shield my lookout, energised my being that finalised the violence the clout

Specialness that taught me lessons and that nothing is impossible you can realise your dreams, whose shining light on the journey we shared led the way as it brightly gleamed

Who was the paddle that kept us afloat through the fjords and the stream, through the days, months and years never gave up or ran out of steam

When we were up against trouble specialness that met it squarely face to face, stopped all the evil that threatened to invade our space

Who was forever focused too quick to be outwitted those demons could catch outpace, a one woman army defeating the enemy until they gave up the chase

Specialness who gifted me the honour of her love and trust, who day after day told me you can do this finish the journey it's a given a must

Grit that fuelled her vision her plans which were so robust, who paved the way to the end of our journey to happiness with her special magical stardust

Weary

I was weary frail and weak, what's up I hear lost your tongue can't speak

Of course I wanted to scream shout at him and shriek, but that's what he wanted so he could flip go for me totally freak

I poured myself yet another drink which was my soldier in this battle war, lit a cigarette waiting to see what would happen would I end up once more on the floor

The times inside I'd think I wish I could go leave forever go through that door, but that was a dream seriously too much to ask for

It was on one of those dark and dreary nights, that a blast from the past came back into sight

It was my childhood friend still full of energy so bright, a specialness that would become my confidante my leading light

I know you are sad she said I totally understand, but I'm here for you to take you away please come take my hand

Don't be scared everything is covered meticulously planned, and so I followed my specialness who took me safely away from my murky past, that wasteland

Voice

I heard a voice that was talking to me it seemed to be singing a redemption song, am I hearing things such comfort and tenderness no it can't be I must be wrong

It was telling me not to give up I was not alone that I must remain strong, and then the voice I heard suddenly materialised and there was the specialness I'd known all along

That voice you heard in your head now stands before you, I'm back my friend I am your courage and strength that will keep you safe get you through

Your darkest days are now gone, your life now I'm back will have a completely different view, and true to her promise she raised me back up brought me happiness my special friend so true

Change

I'm here to make a change she said how you feel inside and outside of your skin, change the way you see yourself bring back the life and soul of you that is deep within

I'm going to change how you see yourself show you that you are not a has been, come my friend it's time to go on a journey so life once more for you can again begin

I'm going to change your sadness and fear to tranquillity and peace, all your broken pieces I will mend so once again you are one piece

I hold the secret combination so the lock on that dark door will open give you the release, and my promise to you forever more the hatred you have endured will cease

I looked at her with love in my heart and my eyes open wide, the thanks for the hope of all she promised I just couldn't hide

Can we, you will help me thank you as the tears flowed that I freely cried, I then took her hand of friendship as she led the way became my guide

So started the changes she promised that I thought were beyond reach, the draining of the blood of life from me no longer taken by that leech

Specialness that changed the streets of my life to that of a beautiful golden beach, specialness that brought the change to me my dreams with the special wisdom she did teach

Hurricane

Specialness that said to me in every heart there's a hurricane a feeling of being washed out to sea, a feeling that a force is pulling you down smothering your gravity

Each door you go to won't open up locked tight and you don't have the key, the walls closing in nowhere to hide resigning yourself to the fact you'll never be free

But where there's a will there's a way and I am that will that will show you the way, to break through those clouds that have always been misty and grey

To lift you back up make you stand tall give you the courage to say, see you later my fear, my murky past time to bid you farewell I'm off to a bright happier new day

Don't Quit

Don't you quit my specialness said, I'm here to replace your doubt, replace the cracks that have developed give you a new coat some fresh grout

This new coating comes with strength and resilience because that's what it's all about, come hell or high water I will change your life, I'll find a way to get you out

Bewildered worn out from the scorn of the years thrown so low and down on my knees, I looked in the mirror a different vision I saw surely that can't be me

See my specialness said there's a new vision a new face that you now can see, a you that you like with a genuine smile I think now is the time to set you free

This journey we both now will share will make your dreams your aim, all the times he's brought you down no longer you yourself will you blame

The throwing of the dice that dictated your moves that were all a sick and twisted game, all that is now gone you now can hold your head high and know you are no longer in the frame

Your heart is now strong your belief the medal the Victoria Cross from your war, the evil has been defeated no way with me would he win or that you would be done for

Come take my hand the time has come for us to giant leapfrog through that golden door, as there lies a lifetime side by side of untold happiness which is what now lies in store

Promised So Much

I would look across at the man that promised me so much, so why was it that I was under his control caught in his clutch

Why are there no smiles or a tender loving touch, I just can't find the answer everything to me is double-dutch

The man who promised to have and to hold until death do us part, but the only thing he has given me are the pieces of my broken heart

There are no vibrant colours only blacks and greys in my abstract work of art, the curtain is now closing my world is falling apart

Although my life was in tatters and completely a mess, I would think back to my childhood with my best friend happy times incredibly yes

That friend I had been searching for year after year no less, until the day I found a photograph omg it was her looking at me wearing a beautiful red dress

Our two souls became reconnected and so too was our bond, and her specialness reached out to me from thousands of miles away across the golden pond

Specialness whose love and loyalty went over above and beyond, specialness with her strength and courage brought an end to his tyranny she's wonderful very special and an incredibly beautiful blonde

How Do You

How do you give thanks to someone for standing by me through thick and thin, for stopping the craziness that had me reeling my head in a spin

Change my feeling of failure, despair and darkness that was my linchpin, mentally and physically exhausted feeling so ugly outside and within

How can there be any words to show the magnitude of where I was to where I am now, the aura of you and your specialness determined to bring me happiness in any way any how

Over the hills and far away so your beautiful specialness did plough, through the miles of our journey I would become weary but you were always there to wipe my brow

There are no words for the enormity of your strength that moved mountains and kept me on track, who parted the seas and set sail with me away from the door behind which was totally pitch black

The mystical fairy dust that closed all the hurt of my cracks, you were on a mission now so was your quest no there would be no way in hell would you let me go back

How do you show someone as beautiful as you all you've taught and given me through the miles together we have tread, no more looking over my shoulder, scared and living in dread

How can I ever thank you for making me safe at peace at night when I am in my bed, and the wonderful times and happiness you've bestowed on me and the happy times that now forever lay ahead

Gifted

I was given the gift of a precious specialness who always held the formulae to my happiness and laughter who was always so carefree

It wasn't always like that as I lived for years alone and drowning in that deep big open sea, until along came her life raft which rescued and unlocked my chains with her magical golden key

A special friendship in knowing not just to hold but how to hold my hand, seeing the messages in my tears no words needed the silence she could see and could fully understand

How she stopped me from sinking and going under in that desert of quicksand, untangling the confusion of our journey the routes and paths she led me through each one with precision she had planned

Whenever I was falling she was there with both arms open wide, gave me the confidence to once again and in myself stand tall and take pride

Who helped me to bury and put my past behind me completely push it aside, stopped me from hating myself so that I was able to look in the mirror and no longer living life having to hide

Specialness who stopped me living life like a robot being controlled with no feelings and no love to feel, piecing my broken heart back together which her loving tenderness did heal

Who opened the door to happiness galore which saw me skip

jump and do a cartwheel, and the specialness that was in her beautiful smile because she knew I had finally found happiness and yes it was real

Can't Be Replaced

Specialness that can't be replaced or captured in a jar, because there is no one else as special as you by far

The ears that were there to listen that unstuck all the unsightly tar, the hands that led and guided me through my journey you are my bright shining star

The mind and heart of your understanding never ever one to judge, whenever I faltered you'd steady me with your kid gloves and a gentle nudge

The miles you walked beside me day after day we would trudge, the constant reminders you were here now and forever no way would you leave or budge

The times you caught my tears whenever I was sad or blue, showed me how when my mixed up mind didn't know how or what to do

Specialness that had the answers when I didn't have a fucking clue, who restored my confidence and strength the catalyst of my breakthrough

To the freedom I had so many years before that I was robbed of and padlocked behind the darkest door, until my specialness with her magical key put my past to bed saying that was your life before

Specialness who gently pieced me back together and lovingly did restore, and found me peace and happiness that I now have thank you my specialness who I just love and adore

Treasure Chest

I found my very own treasure chest as I was floating out to sea, drifting into the wilderness to wash ashore along with my debris

That's when I saw the cask covered in seaweed and at its side a golden key, and couldn't believe what was inside there all for me

It wasn't stacked with diamonds, silver or gold, but something much more special of a story untold

Treasure so special and rare a miracle to behold, it held everything that is my Anam Cara as I will now for you unfold

In there was a picture of us as kids at her birthday party I was sat looking up at her with pride, even at such a young age she was a shining light our leader and our guide

Although in truth not as innocent as the beauty would depict as the torn jeans and mud that she could not hide, precious years in our own adventure land never apart forever side by side

The rest was filled with her special presence that lived in my heart and soul, her courage and strength that broke each chain of the life I lived the violence and control

The unique specialness who then took me on a journey to find complete happiness that was her goal, specialness that is my treasure chest that has made and makes my life whole

Countless Times

The countless times I've tried to thank you for all you've given me and done, the countless messages and verses I've penned none of which have come close not one

But it's hard to say thank you to your specialness that is as bright as the morning sun, there are no words that can express what I want to say to you that very special someone

How can I show you how much you've done for me, it's hard now to remember how damaged and broken I was the only way out was to die only that way could I be free

Specialness that changed all that breathed in new life the vision and belief and who held the magical key, who never left my side protected me as I took those scary steps to be free

Where are the words that can show the days/months/years and hours you took me by the hand, put back the sparkle that had vanished back inside me and all around me that was bland

If I could paint a picture it would be a masterpiece filled with the vibrant colours of your specialness so grand, depict the journey you took me on to that brighter beautiful happier land

I'll keep on writing and trying to find a way that encompasses the specialness of you, how you worked your magic to change me into who I am as only your specialness could do

Of the strength of your specialness that shattered the darkness to let the light come shining back through, I wish I could write and show you my thanks and how special you are through and through

Ray of Sunshine

Specialness that paints gold rays of sunshine wherever she does go, waves her magic wand that gives the atmosphere a brilliant glow

Who can pick up a dandelion and spread such joy as she breathes and then does blow, whose energy is infectious never still up and down like a yo-yo

Everywhere she goes there's a garden filled with flowers colourful as they bloom, fun and laughter a given when you are with her you are always in the playroom

The aura of her specialness that lights up each and every room, sadness with her doesn't exist not a chance there's never darkness or gloom

Specialness that has the psychic insight that reaches inside of you, puts herself aside then steps into your shoes

Who looks then listens patiently thinks things through and through, can see when there is heartache and knows exactly what to do

That is just a little of who and what my specialness brings, there are not enough words or verse that can capture everything

Specialness that makes you feel alive gives you the strength to spread your wings, thank you for being the specialness that is my Anam Cara that I love more than anything

Stopped My Troubles

Specialness that stopped my troubles met them squarely face to face, gave me the strength and determination to never give up the chase

That blew away all my fears and sadness obliterated them to outer space, changed all that into happiness which my world does now embrace

Specialness that showed me never should you give up hope, together with me beside you whatever is thrown our way I promise you we will cope

No more will you falter shake and walk on a tightrope, the moon and stars you can reach for just look through my telescope

Her special vibrant colours surrounded me replaced the black and the grey, and the warmth and brightness of sunshine began to fill all of my days

My inner being stopped being lonely desolate with total dismay, as my specialness led me through the green fields towards the freedom that would become my gateway

Specialness that knew the right roads to take to become who I wanted to be, whose loyalty love and trust went beyond the highest degree

Who moulded the iron to make the key for the door of number thirty-three, looked at me and said this is all for you my friend, you are now truly free

Fragile

Specialness that saw I was fragile didn't know how much more I could take, who saw that I was drowning from the tears that were forming a lake

Who could see the man I lived with was wrong a nasty piece of a snake, who knew she couldn't sit back and do nothing she had to help me before I did break

Specialness that listened to my secrets that broke my heart in two, who spent the hours of each day and night planning how to help me what to do

The endless pacing the countless cups of coffee on the brew, who sat me down and tenderly told me the truth opened my eyes to a completely different view

Specialness with so much patience held my hand with each baby step I trod, who encouraged me as I faltered with her beautiful smile and her knowing nod

That showed me it wasn't my fault I wasn't to blame I definitely was not odd, became my protector to deal with my demons was my very own vice squad

Specialness who in time saw me change and the courage and strength come back to life within, that brought back my genuine smile cheek to cheek is now my grin

Who shared a journey with me eradicated the nightmare that was a sin, led me to the bright light of happiness thank you my beautiful very special Robyn

Rescued

Specialness that rescued me a broken individual after years of mental and physical abuse, from the demon who kept me trapped for each blow there was always an excuse

Who saved me from that ticking time bomb stopped the explosion her specialness was the defuse, her specialness changing my being to the complete opposite of living as a recluse

Baby steps she walked with me each day, each month and through the years, some scary they seemed to be giant leaps but my specialness took away all of my fears

Specialness that was the handkerchief and bucket that captured all of my tears, and despite the miles between us always knew when I needed her as her BOO would magically appear

And as we walked together into the great unknown, not knowing what lay ahead what would be in our zone

Determination fuelled her in her quest to get me to her milestone, to safety and happiness no longer in darkness scared and alone

Specialness that encouraged me to look in the mirror to once again love the person of my reflection, her specialness that got me to stop blaming myself end the self-dejection

Who gave me back my confidence vision and belief that changed my dull complexion, beautiful specialness that took me from a living nightmare to happiness specialness that brought an end to my disconnection

The Artist

Specialness that became my artist a new beginning she painted for me, my being needed restoring it was tarnished and dusty the colours you could no longer see

She gathered up her cloths and her brushes this wouldn't be easy no-one would disagree, but she had all the love and patience needed together with her special creativity

She thought back to our childhood and the friend of the years she shared, she could see there was a fear before her as it was evidence for years no one had given any love or cared

Sadness of the carefree friend she had so much fun with always together they were paired, how had she faded to such dullness become so timid and scared

A master at her craft so her quest began, firstly deep solid strokes then her brush sweeping as softly as only she can

After a while the colours started to return and merge together into a vibrant span, the life coming back with the strength to finally stand up to that violent horrible man

Not quite finished it needed a last special touch just a little bit more, bold bright colours to get right to the heart and into the core

And so the life came back into me that my specialness did graciously lovingly restore, her greatest masterpiece freeing me into an abundance of happiness that had been so lost through the years of before

For Years and Years

For years and years I lived a life that I thought was the norm, the reality that I couldn't see was that I was stuck in the middle of a thunderstorm

All my being who I was had gone away my personality deformed, but I couldn't see how much the girl I was had changed was lost had been transformed

Routine became my existence of the days that formed into the years, fear of when I came home what lay behind the door if I didn't do his bidding to his wishes adhere

Murky mist and sadness was my existence my surrounding sky my sphere, memories of home where good times and happiness filled all of my yesteryears

Back then I had a vision so many dreams and opportunities when he put on my wedding ring, how different to the life we would share a nice house kids a beautiful garden where the birds would flock and sing

I held onto the saying you never know what tomorrow will bring, a miracle could happen take me away from the darkness stop the horrible deadly daily sting

That miracle it did happen the answer to my prayers, my childhood special friend reappeared large as life and with my secrets I did share

Her specialness worked it's magic freeing me from his control she was a force that nothing could compare, specialness who put my pieces back together and my life that she so lovingly did repair

Another Day Over

Another day over as I step through that unsightly door, my stomach is churning and I feel sick and rotten to the core
Wondering what I would be faced with no idea what would be in store, I pray for some peace and not the yelling of orders before going into the battle of war
As always I would smile ask how his day had been hoping that would keep the peace, I would try to be upbeat talk about my day so his anger would subside and decrease
But it was the same old same old the nightmare never did or could cease, another day closing and along with that another missing piece

One evening I went out into the garden and saw something so beautiful so free, wishing I could change places wishing that I could fly and that was me
Wanting to know the secret could I catch it as I tried chasing it around the tree, but it was far too quick as it enchantingly moved a gracious wonder to behold to see
A beautiful dragonfly its radiant colours of yellow green orange purple and blue, it then came buzzing towards me and landed right in front of my shoe
It then spread its wings the colours blinding me and then there stood before me was a beautiful view, it was my specialness back to save me who took my hand and off to happiness we both soared and flew

Safety Net

Searching for a safety net to catch me when I fall, to stop the punches and the kicks when he fancied to have a brawl

The please don't, it hurts, stop it all the pleas that I did call, were never heard it only stopped when the flame went out of his fireball

Nowhere to run to nowhere to turn, my only release was to go to work put food on the table my chains were securely tied, gone were the hopes and dreams of a happy life as I took my vows as the blushing bride

Going from that to a hunger for a life that had now sadly died, praying and hoping one day I'll find someone to trust and in whom I can confide

And then my prayers were answered to what I had clung onto the hope, that someone would come and find me before I reached the end of my tightrope

A specialness that came back into my life to wash away all my fears and gave me the courage to stand tall and cope, brought the life and colour back into me just like a kaleidoscope

Specialness that opened up her soul to mine, became the backbone to my tethered weathered spine

Her x-ray vision that saw and read all the warning signs, who took me away from that life to the serenity of my happiness that is now my new coastline

Presence

I'm surrounded by a presence so magical, a specialness that is a gift, that came and heard my soul calling knew I was just keeping afloat was all adrift

Who saw the makeup I was wearing needed a new coat a brand new facelift, who read the signs of my secrets the truth that was my darkness my rift

A specialness that took my hand in friendship and showed me there was a way, that sunshine could come back and brighten my each and every day

Who showed me how to dance again with the grace of a beautiful ballet, and led me to a happier place so no longer did I have to hope and pray

Window Pane

Looking through the window pane the rain is bucketing down, just like the years of tears I've shed I'm surprised I haven't yet drowned

Trying to find some answers as I put on my dressing gown, holding onto cherished memories from an age ago miles away in a different town

Back then the sun was always shining happiness filled all those carefree days, dreams created to chase and fulfil come whatever come what may

All that was lost and gone when I pulled up and parked in a different driveway, the beginning of the control of my nightmare the start of the rot the decay

The house from the outside was lovely so inviting until you opened the door, it was bland barren and dark had no carpet on the floor

In the corner was a chair and on it sat a solitary figure who would look then the menacing would outpour, and later all the secrets would be gathered and locked up and placed in a drawer

I held onto the hope of the years gone by but I wasn't sure how much longer my strength would last, then came a magnificent lightning bolt of a presence from my happier past

My childhood friend was back her strength and courage was mighty strong and vast, who gathered me up rescuing me destroying all of my nightmare of the demons with one incredible very special almighty blast

Inside I Scream

'You okay' he asks 'yes I'm fine' I say but inside is the opposite
that I scream, I look at the man before me that has sold me down
the river into the stream

How can you stand there as though nothing has happened no
remorse not seeing it as it would seem, the only thing I have to
thank you for is destroying my being my dream

And then he turns to self-pity his health issues of course they
are the reason the blame, why he changes from Mr Nice Guy to
the one that becomes so angry his persona it does inflame

I'll get help he says it won't happen again I believe him but
it's just once again mind games, I hope this time things will
change but as the years rolled by of course everything remained
the same

I was at my lowest stood at the edge of that dark black hole ready
to jump down, when I heard a familiar voice saying I'm back and
I stopped myself and instead I turned around

There stood my childhood best friend no it can't be as
bewildered I looked at her with a frown, and then her presence
and beautiful smile lit up the room yes it is her she has come back
her graciousness is back in this town

Opening the door with her magical key she led me out into
the night, guided by the stars which brightened our path she held
my hand so tenderly and tight

Together sharing a journey with each baby step we took

disappearing was my fear and my fright, until the dark clouds of my past did clear into the life of happiness her specialness took me one so wonderful and bright

Pray for Sleep

So many times I would pray for sleep but that would never come, I would end up creeping down the stairs with my heart beating like a drum

I would make a coffee smoke a cigarette sit in the dark so alone and glum, and then I would hear a noise turn around startled and then be struck completely numb

Nowhere was I safe that dark cloud followed me wherever I would go, if I wasn't at home then there would be phone calls and text messages and all I wanted to do was scream oh no

But instead I would pretend everything was fine couldn't be better yes of course you know, the mask and the false smile was the greatest act in that crazy mad and manic show

I knew the scenes and my lines totally off by heart, but I didn't want to be in that show I wanted to be able to play a different part

Night after night the sad story I would tell I'd get the odd clap as the audience did depart, and then I would remove my makeup and hope tomorrow would be better that it would bring about a new start

Then one night as I bent to pick my bag up, I heard a voice say time to go my lovely to star in a new show in a different town, the tears flowed down my face at the sound of the voice from my past and her beautiful presence as I turned around

Come we need to go shopping for some new makeup and a beautiful gorgeous new gown, and then my specialness took me on a journey where all along the way happiness she flagged down

Potter's Wheel

The potter's wheel is spinning round and round so fast, the sculpture concentrating on the outlines of the creation before him that he had cast

He was making changes it had to be perfect in his eyes had to be his typecast, he was nearly finished now it was as he wanted a completely different contrast

The cast was that of a young girl so innocent with the world at her feet, who met a young guy who promised her the world he was generous and ever so sweet

They got married to have and to hold and moved to their dream home in a lovely street, and from that moment on started the violence, the control and the deceit

Each day he would spin his wheel and at her cast he would chip away, not quite to his satisfaction tirelessly he would craft and model the clay

The young girl was now older misshaped her pallor was sadness and completely grey, until he woke up one morning his wheel had stopped spinning it wouldn't work that day

There was a new spinning wheel with a presence tendering the clay with love and with care, it was the young girl's childhood friend who was sat there on the sculptor's chair

The tools she used were her gentleness her loving heart working changing the shape of her nightmare, and when she finished ending the years that he had shaped her final touch putting a genuine smile to replace what had been her despair

Just When

Just when I was at my lowest and could only see the way out was to end it all, a beautiful specialness came to me and stopped my fatal fall

Whose soul heard the silent shrieks of my despair my desperate calls, smashed through my prison wall like a mighty fireball

Specialness who could see behind the mask the sadness written all over me, the truth of my life I couldn't hide which she could clearly see

Who for hours sat with me as I shared my secrets catching my tears and holding my hands so tenderly, and made me a promise to piece me back together make me once again happy and carefree

Specialness who showed me what was right and the life I was living was wrong, that happiness was not about living in fear like a rabbit staring at danger headlong

That I had a choice and could follow my dreams not live by his rules all day long, that inside of me there was a heartbeat and a wonderful beautiful song

And so we shared a journey and with each baby step her specialness fought the control and the constant of his flack, fiercely protecting me so no longer was I in danger under attack

Until the day came when she said look we've arrived we are now on the right track, and from that day forward she gifted me true happiness with no more nightmares no going back

Pain

The pain pierces through my being as all around me my world is falling apart, the depression has taken its hold on me it's too strong and way too smart

It's a constant cloud that hangs over me and causes the pounding in my heart, as the sweat pours out of me I plead with it to go, please depart

But it doesn't hear me as I take a deep breath before I can step out of that door, my palms are wet and my legs are shaking I have to pace myself slowly so I don't fall to the floor

And after a while the fear subsides a little just when I thought I could take no more, and then into my car I go to work and hope there will be no further attacks in store

What brought all this on was the life which I lived to the man who I married who promised me the earth, I got the complete opposite a fist full of dollars any time any place can you believe even after I had given birth

There was always an excuse why it happened but deep down it was his satisfaction his mirth, daily was the control lies deceit and false promises that was all I was worth

That was then but this is now as I am now mentally and physically in a better place, thanks to the specialness in my life who eradicated him from every inch of my space

Specialness who read into my soul and took hold of my nightmare never giving up the chase, which is why I now live life in happiness and peace with a constant genuine smile on my face

A Special Presence

There is a very special presence which is distinctive and very unique, which I am blessed to have in my life which surrounds me so life is never dull or bleak

Specialness who stood firm beside me despite the nightmare I was caught in and who didn't turn the other cheek, specialness with strength and courage she is a powerhouse and is beautifully mystique

Who came back into my life to take control opening up my secret and then stopped my living nightmare, specialness who stood resilient and firm no matter what he tried this was one individual he just couldn't scare

Specialness who took me on a journey holding my hand to a new life guiding my baby steps that got me there, specialness who is a wonderment so gracious, kind caring a beautiful specialness so precious and rare

Imagine

Imagine living in a world of sadness where darkness is your only light, where there is no sparkle nothing no happiness left to ignite

Where you have to live with a secret that's sinister and not quite right, and feeling all your strength and hope seeping out of you losing all the will to fight

Can you imagine living with a shadow that will never leave you alone, it follows you everywhere steps into your shoes so you are never on your own

To have your existence changed and moulded to become a different clone, and never get to feel tenderness have to live each day where love is never shown

But that wasn't in my imagination that was the life I lived which I had, nowhere to go and no one to turn to, I was a lonely frightened nomad

No one had any idea of the truth they would think you're joking you are mad, until one day presence heard my soul calling and could see the truth and just how bad

Specialness who came back into my life who imagined a different life for me, who made a vow and a promise that one day she would from his clutches set me free

Who had a vision of blue skies with birds singing I would be happy in peace and tranquillity, specialness who broke down my prison walls and took me on a journey to what she imagined which every day I now live to see

I Used To Be

I used to be so carefree so happy but then sadness took a hold, every day I lived in the dark my eyes permanently covered by a blindfold

I never felt the warmth I was always shivering always felt cold, because of a shadow who was my constant and my every move it completely controlled

I would paint a mask on my face which through the day I would have to wear, I would go out and earn a living but there was no escape its presence was always there

Every minute of every hour it would hound me making sure that I was aware, that this life would be forever and that in no one my secret would I ever be able to share

Every day became a routine my goal would be for another day to get through, when I look back at some of the darkest times how I did I just don't have a clue

I was growing weak my strength seeping out of me as my nightmare grew and grew, until one day as I drew back the curtains I looked out to a completely different view

The sun was shining brightly the flowers vibrant all fully in bloom, I looked all around me and I was stood in a different place, in a different room

And then I heard a familiar voice of my special friend saying we did it my lovely put paid to the past the doom and gloom, the specialness of her who freed me giving me back my true self and happiness which each day I now do consume

Gift

Specialness that has a gift and talent that can make your dreams come true, who can find the positive inside the negative then paint a picture with a completely different view

Who no matter how much you try to hide can see the pain which you are going through, specialness who wipes that all away with her beautiful smile and makes the grey skies blue

Her wisdom is faultless and she can always see through to the other side, who tenderly allays all your fears so no longer your secrets you have to continually hide

Specialness who with strength and courage faced his adversity took it all in her stride, specialness who then led me to my happiness peace and tranquillity forever brushing my nightmare aside

Living in a World

Imagine living in a world when the night falls on you and you know what is coming next, and no matter what you try to say and do it has no effect on the vent and the vex

Night time should be a peaceful time not an eruption of rage that leaves you feeling baffled and in total perplex, having to live with the knowledge you were living with someone with whom you had no respect

Then the next day you would have to face the world as if nothing had happened at all, having to hide the bruises inflicted by someone who makes your skin crawl

Having to live with the guilt keeping it a secret feeling so ashamed and feeling small, and ever so lonely and weary no one to catch you every time you did stumble and fall

Each day living with so many questions muddled up inside your head, no one to help find you the answers just the constant living in dread

Waking up to grey skies not knowing what the day would bring what lay ahead, well I do because that was my life before someone special gifted me a new life instead

Specialness who I told my secrets who was the one with whom I finally could confess, who found my missing pieces healed my open wounds and ended all of my distress

Who took me on a journey away from my nightmare and onwards to what would be the future success, of a world where I now live in peace happiness and tranquillity which my specialness for me did find did bless

Guide and Protect

Specialness who guides and protects me never fails to catch me as I am about to fall, who has a psychic phenomenon that can hear the silent pleas my soul does call

Who has a presence that is my protector and is my warmth and loving shawl, specialness who reaches into my heart and being never failing to make me feel ten feet tall

Specialness whose mystical magic surrounds you making each day a living fairy-tale, and whatever lies ahead what goal there is to there achieve with her beside you, you know you will never fail

Whatever storms there are ahead she will pull you through and get you back on track and on the right trail, the beautiful specialness of her who brought me out of my nightmare to the happiness I now each day do inhale

Turn To

Specialness I could turn to and who became my greatest gift, who gathered me up from my nightmare tenderly saving me and my soul she did uplift

The chains that I was locked in she broke and aside she did shift, and stopped me joining the darkness where I was going towards where I was beginning to drift

Specialness who saw the tears in my eyes and how lonely I was and oh so sad, who unscrambled all my insecurities stopped me from going insane and totally mad

Who knew inside there were secrets some which were ugly and bad, whose deepest wish was to bring back her carefree friend and untold happiness to add

The specialness of her who opened her arms saying come my friend don't be ashamed to cry, I am here to catch your tears until they no longer fall they become dry

I can see the dark side too and I'm here to take you on a journey so one day you can wave it goodbye, and so I placed my trust in her specialness in which I knew I could rely

No longer was I standing at the crossroad not knowing which path to take what to do, specialness who held my hand as she walked beside me saying I'll never leave I promise I will stand by you

Specialness who turned my darkness to light and the grey skies to blue, and onwards to a new life of happiness thanks to her specialness so wonderful and true

Worthwhile

Specialness who changed my expression from sadness to a beaming genuine smile, who changed my persona my DNA and the whole of my profile

No longer do I have the weight of the world on my shoulders as each day once they used to pile, all because of the specialness who came back and opened my eyes to why life was worth living and worthwhile

Specialness who took away all of my fear as onwards on our journey together that day we stepped through that door, whose encouragement kept me going through the times I thought I couldn't take anymore

Who found me a new home with new surroundings open fields all for me to explore, specialness who replaced my darkness with the light of happiness which are now the only showers each day onto me which do pour

Frightened

The girl stood frightened and frozen paralysed by his eerie and sinister stare, so many words left unspoken of what was to come was there written in his glare

Silently inside her heart was pleading asking him for once no don't this time some love instead please share, but he couldn't hear her and yet again she fell and was trapped in his snare

After it was all over she would hear the 'I'm sorry it won't happen again', shaken and stirred so many mixed emotions would race through her brain

She would check upon her kids they were still asleep thankfully they hadn't seen or heard her pain, and then her tears would flow and fall like the rain

She was lost, lonely and broken in a world of no choices not any she was able to see, and the life she lived was a secret locked tightly in a drawer and each door secure there was no key

Many a time she would ask herself how did this happen come to this from once being so happy and carefree, it's incredible looking back at the lost soul of that girl because that girl was once me

What happened to change all of that to the life I am blessed to live in now, it was because of a very special person who came back into my life and I'll tell you how

Her specialness could see through me into my soul read the truth of my secrets and made a very special vow, which was to take me on a journey to end my nightmare gifting me my freedom and happiness which only her specialness into my life will now allow

No Room To Be Sad

Specialness who listened as I shared a secret and gave me a tender loving hug, who released the dust of the dirt for years which I had swept under that age old rug

Who didn't sit back to judge or think I was and had been a complete and utter mug, who instead dived deep into the water in which I was drowning and with a great heave released the pressure and pulled the plug

Specialness who gave back the positive attitude and qualities which when I was young I had, who showed me kindness caring devotion and love the complete opposite to the many years which had been so bad

Who proved me wrong when she said I could start a new life be free I thought she was stark raving mad, specialness who gave me a wonderful reason to live and who smothers my every day in happiness no longer is there any room now for me to be sad

Gold

She has a heart of gold graciousness and specialness with which nothing can compare, she fills this world with love joy and happiness wherever she is it fills the air

To all of those she loves she gives her specialness it's ours with which to share, whenever you feel vulnerable frightened or alone her presence is always there

Specialness which knows no bounds whether it is night or day, who will always make sure she will wash all of your troubles away

The specialness of all of that who picked me up saved me from the nightmare guided me on the right pathway, her specialness who diminished all of my paranoia knowing how lucky I am to have such her specialness and more forever which is here to stay

Here and Now

Specialness who crossed the waters and travelled thousands of miles, who came back into my life with her graciousness and beautiful smile
Who would be the catalyst to change my life opened up that locked turnstile, and show me that yes life was worth living it was indeed worthwhile
It's hard to imagine the years which have flown by, caught in a world and control the only rule is to comply
Being the target of violence and obscenities it was the only way him I could satisfy, exhausted by the countless unanswered questions and constantly left wondering why

How could I escape how could that ever change well it did and I'll tell you how, what was the reason of the change from my nightmare to the freedom for years he did disallow
It came in the form of my very special friend who could read my soul and into my mind and so she did plough, which is why I am here today in the here and now
Specialness who could see through his façade who failed to make her run for the hills, she was too strong her armour made of steel through it he just could not drill
Who stood firm wore him down made him swallow his own bitter pill and who then took me on a journey to happiness a promise she made which she did fulfil

Until

I thought I had lost the will to live totally given up the fight, that was until a specialness came back into my life bringing back into it the light

Specialness who could read between the lines into my soul she reached and made it her vow for me to fight, and through the weeks months and years ahead she restored my belief and my sight

The journey we shared was far from easy many obstacles were thrown our way, but she overcame and deflected them much to his frustration and dismay

Each day she held my hand tightly her strength and courage got me through each and every day, until we reached the end of the road where all of my troubles her specialness washed away

Puzzle

My life is a puzzle with pieces missing especially from inside,
and the pieces left are what he has carved since the day I walked
down the aisle and became his bride

I know there's a different world out there where happiness
is shared yes somewhere there outside, but of course there is no
escape for me, as there is no door left open wide

He's changed my life around how I live think and breathe,
my mind is so mixed up from the lies and the clever way he does
deceive

He knows every trick in the book one step ahead got
everything up his sleeve, and how he loves to give me that snide
look and smile which tells me you're mine you'll never leave

He thought he'd hid my missing pieces that I could not be
put back together again, that he would be forever my umbrella
because never would there be sunshine only rain

His victory call was loud and clear forever would he be king
the one to reign, but he didn't account for a magical specialness
that would soon come and his empire she would slain

Specialness who found my missing pieces each one she
tenderly slotted back into place, leaving him bewildered as he
thought they could never be found there could be no trace

Specialness who outwitted him and the demons of his
nightmare and rat race, who raised me from the ashes of his
destruction and led me to a new wonderful and happier place

Specialness

Specialness who can put a smile on your face even though you are torn and broken inside, who can bring you back from the brink so no longer you run or have to hide

Whose magic can dry up all of your tears so no longer they flow like a tide, and with her special kindness caring graciousness and giving is always there with arms open wide

Specialness who single handedly when she knew of my secret went on a crusade, to restore the life back into me bring back the colour into my life that was worn and had begun to fade

Who painted a picture of a new life a masterpiece to me she portrayed, and whose specialness to my old life and a happier one she so beautifully did trade

Seven Letters

Seven letters that spell the word 'stopped' which is synonymous to the specialness in my life and what she gave to me, who stopped the nightmare I had been living in for years who released and set me free

Specialness who put a stop to my hurt and pain swept away each particle of my debris, who opened the gateway to a journey we shared with her special and magical key

Specialness who held my hand with each baby step we took, whose caring tenderness and love calmed me as I shivered and as I shook

Who stopped the negativity and instead taught me how to search for positive for that always to look, specialness who wrote new chapters of an adventure a wonderment fairy-tale ending to my book

Specialness who stopped the tears with her sunshine which for years did flow, who ended the dark misty murky clouds with her beautiful bright shining glow

Who stopped the tyranny of the obscenities and violence which at me he constantly did throw, and gave me the answers to the questions for years I just didn't know

Specialness who came back and changed my whole being and turned my world upside down, whose boundless energy fun and gaiety un-creased my weary frown

Who broke down his barriers of the fortress of his kingdom so in its own waters it did drown, specialness who stopped my circus of despair so I could emerge as a carefree and happy clown

Can't be Real

This can't be real surely as I wake up there's no tenseness in the air, I look all around me waiting to be greeted by that fearful and eerie glare

To see the anger bubbling and the hatred contained there in his stare, I search and rub my eyes no it isn't it's no longer there

I go into the kitchen to make myself a coffee waiting to hear some obscenity, for another piece to be taken stripped from my being, my identity

To be followed around my every move watched cocooned with that man so ugly so beastly, but his presence has gone it's just me on my own I'm now rid of him I have complete serenity

And then I look to my mantelpiece at the freedom photo and that beautiful smile, the specialness I now have in my life so gracious caring and gentile

It's my very special friend who changed my existence brought me a whole new lifestyle, whose loyalty devotion protection and courage went far further than an extra mile

Specialness who read the silence of my despair and pain living in the control of that man, who could read him like a book see right through him how his mind worked every inch she did scan

Who stood firm and outwitted all his games destroyed each of his every plan, which is why I'm now safe and in a happier place specialness who said dare to dream because you know you can